This book belongs to:

____

Diversity

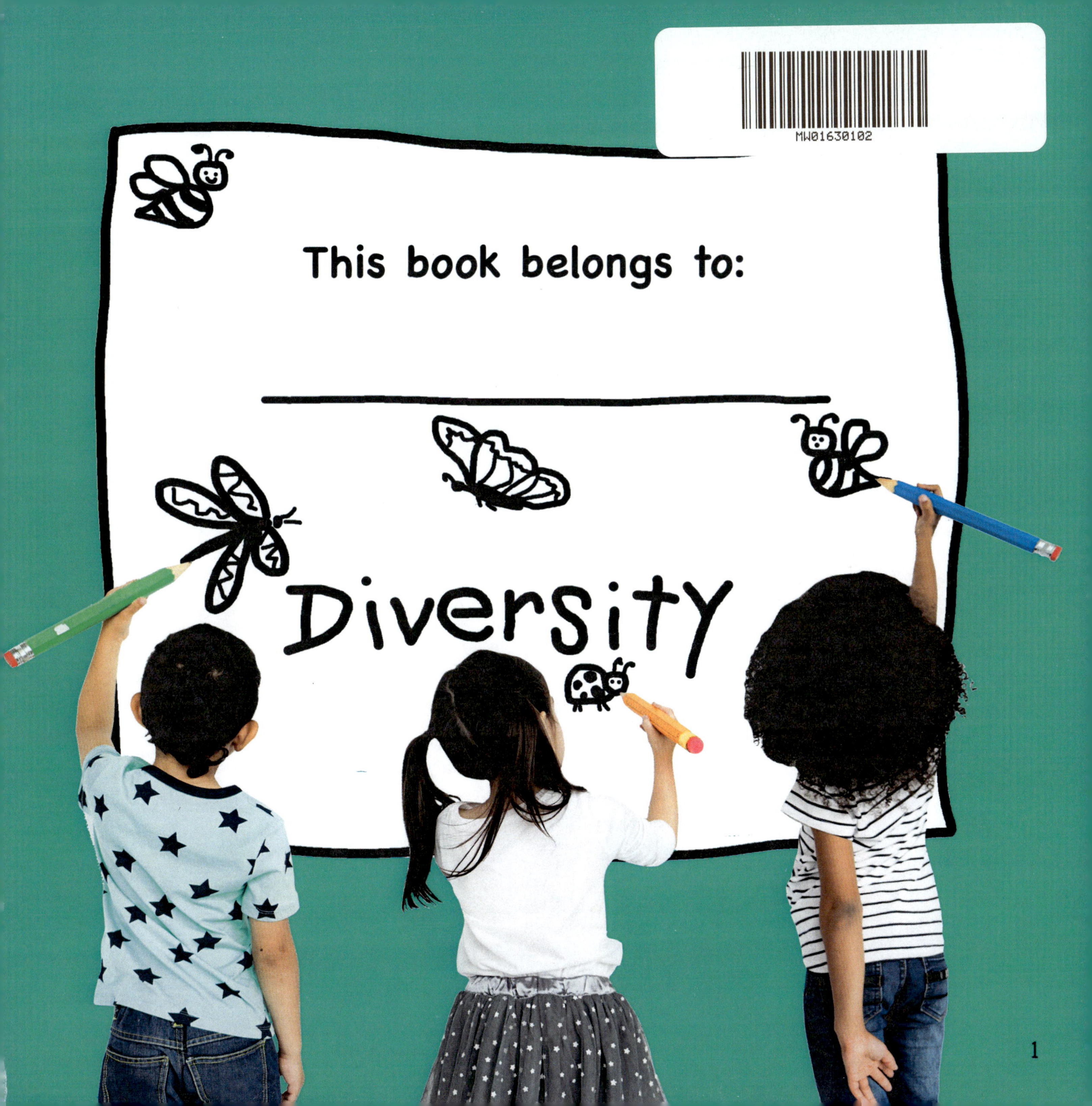

Dedication
For God, who made us "fearfully and wonderfully" diverse; my husband and Irish inspiration, Desmond Finbarr Nolan; and all the children willing to accept, be kind to, and make friends with kids who are not like them, no matter where they come from or what they look like.

Allia Zobel Nolan

Acknowledgement
To my friend, associate, and book designer extraordinere, Mary pat Pino, who believed in this project and gave it her all... huge thanks.

What I Like About YOU
A Book About Acceptance

Copyright © 2019 by Allia Zobel Nolan
Published by AlliaWrites, Norwalk, Connecticut 06851
ISBN 978-0-578-57266-6

Line drawings, cover, and book design by Mary pat Pino
Mary pat Design, Westport, Connecticut 06880

Photos by shutterstock.com and istock.com

What I Like About YOU

A Book About Acceptance

By
Allia Zobel Nolan

Sequel to the bestseller and Mom's Choice Award Winner,
What I Like About Me: A Book Celebrating Differences
For more titles, visit www.AlliaWrites.com

Just for You:

Imagine a world where all kids looked alike—every boy looked and dressed like every other boy, and every girl looked the same from head to toe. Bor—ring? You bet.

I think differences are what make things interesting, fun, and exciting. And if you're like me, when you meet a new girl or boy, you're all questions. I ask things like: Do you play soccer, basketball, baseball? What do you like to eat best? (I love pizza and cookie dough ice cream.) Do you think dogs drool and cats rule...or the other way around? And on and on and on.

Oh, and I just love finding out about different cultures, different ways of life, different foods, though I do draw the line at eating octopus (Ewwww!) I don't know if I'll ever be able to go to countries where some of my new friends grew up or lived. But I feel like I'm in some way connected to these places because I have a friend who has. Plus I learn lots of neat stuff about the world I might not have if I closed myself up like a turtle in a shell.

Okay, sometimes I get scared meeting new people. But then, I take a deep breath and put on a smile, and before you know it, my new friend and I are giggling ourselves silly.

That's why I wrote this book—to introduce you to kids who may look different, but who, once you get to know them, can make the very best of friends. I wrote about why my new friends are special to me. Now it's your turn. I've left a page at the end of the book for you to write about your friends.

Just for Parents, Grandparents, Teachers, Friends:

The kids in **What I Like About You** are all different. And that's why I feature them in this book. Introducing children at a young age to others who aren't their mirror image, opens up their mind to new experiences, makes them feel more comfortable with other cultures/ways of life, and helps them understand that, basically, deep down, we are all pretty much the same.

You may remember my previous book, **What I Like About Me** focused on teaching children self-esteem—to accept and celebrate one's own worth. This new title, **What I Like About You,** goes a step further and teaches youngsters tolerance—to accept and celebrate the worth of others. It highlights the fact that everyone has something to offer.

I feel this is a vital life lesson children need to hear so they don't readily fear and shun others, fall into preconceived notions, and fail to form their own opinions of the new friends they'll met.

As such, it is the perfect timely tool for parents, teachers, grandparents, and clergy who want to get youngsters to respect and appreciate the people around them. I hope you'll enjoy reading this to/with your favorite child as much as I enjoyed writing it.   AZN

The world would be a boring place,
If everyone was the same race.
I love your smile. I love your hair.
If you were blue, I wouldn't care.

Your accent was a nice surprise.
I learned your "chips" are our French fries.
I like that your TV's a "telly."
I love that your jello is "jelly."

You're not like me. But it's okay.
That's why I like you anyway.
I like new words I learn from you.
"Hola!" means "Hi!" and "Hello!" too.

I really like the food you eat.
And chopsticks, boy, they're super neat.
I use them to eat rice and fish.
But octopus (Ewww!) ... is not my dish.

You're always happy, seldom blue.
I'm glad that I am friends with you.
I like that in a little while,
you'll do something to make me smile.

You came from a warm, island place.
I still see sunshine in your face.
You two don't brag. You never shout.
That's not what you are all about.

I love that you wear "geeky" glasses.
And get straight "A's" in all your classes.
You never hide that you are smart.
That's why I liked you from the start.

Who wouldn't like the clothes you wear?
Your Sari sparkles, floats on air.
Some day, maybe you'll lend me one.
We'll look like twins. Won't that be fun?

Because you cover up your head,
mean kids make fun of you, you said.
I like that you don't get upset.
You just ignore it and forget.

Some kids think saying "grace" is odd.
I like that you take time for God.
You're not embarrassed when they tease.
It's God, not them, you want to please.

You taught me things I didn't know.
That's how we make our friendship grow.
Now I can make the dreidel spin.
Watch out, because I'm going to win!

I love the fact you took my dare—
that I could outrun your wheelchair.
You slowed down, though, and let me pass.
As friends go, you sure are first-class.

We celebrated "Be Kind" week.
You two taught me some words to "speak."
I feel so happy knowing you.
Now I can sign "I love you," too.

September is National Deaf Awareness Month
BE KIND
SCHOOL

I like the fact that you don't care
what people think of your red hair.
Your freckles set you miles apart.
To me, you are a work of art.

You're wacky in a different way.
We have a good time when we play.
I like that you have a big heart.
When bullies laugh, you take my part.

21

READ

You always say: "Why should I mind
where people come from if they're kind?"
I guess that's how we all should act.
That's why I like you... that's a fact.

My friend ______________________
is: ☐ nice   ☐ funny   ☐ kind
     ☐ smart   ☐ friendly

My friend ______________________
is: ☐ nice   ☐ funny   ☐ kind
     ☐ smart   ☐ friendly

My friend _______________
is: ☐ nice   ☐ funny   ☐ kind
     ☐ smart   ☐ friendly

My friend _______________
is: ☐ nice   ☐ funny   ☐ kind
     ☐ smart   ☐ friendly

My friend ___________________
is: ☐ nice ☐ funny ☐ kind
☐ smart ☐ friendly

My friend ___________________
is: ☐ nice ☐ funny ☐ kind
☐ smart ☐ friendly

One Last Thing:
Want the author to come visit your
school/library/church/preschool?
Want to buy copies in bulk?
Please email AlliaZobelNolan@gmail.com

The
End

One dollar from the sale of
each book will be donated to the
Catherine Violet Hubbard Animal Sanctuary.

Located in Newtown, Connecticut, CVH's mission
is to enrich the lives of all beings by promoting
compassion and acceptance through programs that
honor the human-animal bond.

Learn more at:
https://cvhfoundation.org/

Made in United States
North Haven, CT
30 September 2024

58126800R00020